LISTENING

LISTENING

Lois Ann Rooney

Copyright © 2020 Lois Ann Rooney

All Rights Reserved by the author, Lois Ann Rooney. No part of this book may be reproduced or recreated without permission of the author. This book contains no advice written or implied. The author and publisher do not assume or entertain any liabilities of this publication as a result of any usage of contents fictional or otherwise (by public or private individuals).

STAR #121212

ISBN-13: 978-1-9409-27-190

MAJOR STAR PUBLISHING

Imprint of Quincentennial Publishing Company

www.majorstar.us

A LIGHT OMNI MEDIA PRODUCTION

Published in the United States of America

Major Star
Publishing

Cover & Jacket design: John Errigo, Ph.D.

Cover design photos: Lois Rooney

Release date: 1 February 2020 | **Second Pressing** 18-2

Dedication

This book of prose
is dedicated to the fine art of

Listening

Not just the simple act of being able to hear
what is being said.
But perceiving what is there before you and
being felt in one's heart.

So, open your spirit and mind

and come

Begin with me

Listening

"Seek the joy that surrounds you ... draw yourself in and hear that wee small voice that gives you direction in life to go on....

LISTENING"

"Do not fear life's changes for they are all around you.....to learn from these things .....and take time to begin.....

LISTENING"

I am not Superman

From where I sit this morning
My window view shrouded by the clouds
I can really begin to think here
and spell these thoughts out loud

Doing all for others the ways I always do
My choice of heart to love all
This is the grand design for you

So, I flounder once and a while
I tumble and I fall
I push back hard with all my might
And again, I rise
See I can do it all

Some days when it's quiet
And alone I sit
Tears of the day fall silently
Just for the spite of it

They are not tears of weakness
Just emotion too hard to hold
So, as I wipe the tears all away
I do so, feeling bold

I will embrace this challenge
This new journey I am on

And to come back stronger
Stronger than the strong
For there is a lot of things to do
and the road ahead is long

I may not be super hero
Though I maybe to those I love
We all stand here together
We fit so hand in glove

So today I start my day a new
As the sky begins to clear
And I thank my God above
For I'm glad I'm still here

We're off to Neverland

Come fly with me, he said
Take my hand
And on this day, we'll fly
I know place to play all day
it's far across the sky

Who are you? I did whisper
Why should I follow you?
I am the fun side you see
of what's inside of you

Wearily I gazed at him
Fun? I shrugged
More like work, I said
lowering my gaze

Yes, I am fun
Remember?
Those lost
and carefree days

I slowly did reach out my hand
And took his in my grasp
Away we flew in the night air
Its coolness made me gasp

We flew past stars
and clouds and things

and headed off to the right
We were high above the tallest tower
and heading for daylight

I'll show a land of wonderment
Of fountains and of shores
Where we can splash the day away
And happiness be yours

I saw that you needed this
He smiled his elvish grin
For I know what it is you need
For I am you closest kin

Little brother you do know my heart
And how to wipe away my cares
I do so love the way you play
and I'll follow you anywhere

I bring you here in gladness
And the love I have for you
Because you you're everything
And I'd be lost without you

Mothers teach your daughters

Mothers teach your daughters
To do as you would do
So, they will stand beside you
And you're so glad they do

Teach them all the lessons
that it took you years learn
The ones they'll want to pass along
When it's for a child they yearn

Allow them to see you stumble
As you make a mistake or two
For it is from these mistakes we make
That comes the lessons due

Let to them see a failure
For many shall there be
But to see you rise above them
Yourself pride is what they'll see

Teach them all of sorrows
For in many forms they come
From loves heartbreak to death grieving
It all come with a sum

Teach them too of compassion
To give from way down deep
That to care for others

Is God's promise
We do keep

Mothers teach your daughters
To be gracious and be kind
To have courage and have wisdom
And hold their hand in thine

For you see it is these lessons
That happen everyday
That we their loving mothers
Will teach and send them on
Their way

I Love a Good Story

I love to watch and hear all the wonderful things
my classmates have done over the years
I applaud their children's successes
And marvel at the fact
most have become grandparents

I love their love stories
Life is a series of challenges
And the backdrop for the greatest of yarns

We love our parents
Except them aging
and becoming more dependent on us
But we were dependent upon them
when we were young

Do always as they ask
For to see them
is to see ourselves

Chloe Chloe

Tiny kitten sitting there
I spy you hiding on the stair
Small and orange with patches of white
You run so fast
Like a flash in the night

Little kitty I hope you know
The joy you bring with hearts in tow
Your golden eyes shine with delight
You purr and play in the warm sunlight

We happily share our home with thee
Our doggy my daughter and oh yes me
From cuddling in my easy chair
To teasing the dog without a care

You run you jump and scamper about
And Lizzy and I yell
"Watch Cat is Out"
The warning is heard as you race round the house
"Don't open the doors
don't let her get out "
Gales of laughter come from all that I love
as we race round the house
to catch her you may need a shove

Over and under around and though
It takes us some time

but we do catch you
And then with a nuzzle
a kiss and a hug
We tell you we love you
You're a slippery little bug

So happy we have you
so happy you are here
For never has a kitten been
so, loved and so dear

Under the rainbow

Under the rainbow
and down the shady lane
I walk with my newest friend
Her name Autumn Rain

Just barely five months of age
This little dog and me
have become quite a pair
and she's special as can be

Our bond we are now forging
As closer we become
For I've allowed her into my heart
to be playful and to run

She is small but she is mighty
Like nothing I have seen
She at times does stand noble
As one sees a queen

But don't let looks deceive you
For behind those shiny eyes
is the devil in the making
She'll keep you mesmerized

Sometimes she can be nippy
Not that it makes it right
But when she's over playing

Look out she just may bite

I'm so glad she came here
To fill the crazy home
For with her close beside me
I don't feel so alone

God has a way in telling you
that the timing is so right
To bring in another little soul
To fill you with delight

He does not leave his love ones
Linger in desperation
For He the great provider
Holds you gently in His care

So, it's with a happy heart I tell of
Our newest doggy dear
I'm thrilled that she is family
and that she is always here

Of ancient blood she comes from
And there is wisdom in her eyes
Perhaps there is a princess
wrapped up in her tiny size

Spying that Bridge

As Autumn and I were walking
As in the we always do
I spied a glimpse of heaven
And now I know it's true

I was thinking of my loved ones
Who are gone from me this day
and wonder I
How they're doing
And is it really like they say?

That's when I saw it
Just off to the right
As the sun began to rise
A gentle arch of color bright
And much to my surprise
It brought a tear into my weary eyes
And was a welcome sight

Was this the Almighty's way of telling
That's everything's ok
For me to keep moving forward
Keep going on my way

So, when it is you wonder if
It's real or is it true
That's when
You'll get an answer

You see the signs from a mighty hand
Just as He wants you to

So, look up when you are walking
For you too just may spy that bridge
It'll be there for just a moment
A little tiny smidge

But it a way of knowing
That everything's ok
And that love is waiting
Forever and a day

Listening

The first real winds of winter are breathing their way
down the street this morning
As the last red maple leaf struggles to hang on to its
branch
Shaking and trembling in the breeze

The house is barely stirring with the sounds of the lives
within
A puppy's sigh
A faintly heard kitten's mew
A closing door
A light switch turning off

From the floor below the sound of crying in the dark
Tears for a life that was
For a life that is
For Family

Listening to these sounds is a profound way
Of understanding
Who we are
What we do
And why

Listening to the conversations
that come from both near and far
That in some respect have greater meaning now than
ever before

It is the ability to not just hear what is said
but to
Listen

Do we listen?

Or are we randomly choosing only to hear what it is
that is most pleasant
And to cleave to that

From house sound to idle prattle it is what we hear in
the course of a day
Or a life
Take time to not just hear
But open our hearts and minds and

Listen

To the wanton cries of a new born child
To the pain and emotion filled laments of our aging
family members

Who not only cry for themselves
but for their beloved families
and the lives they once had
to partners they miss so desperately
And children still in their charge

Listen to the songs of your past

To the stories of you
To the tales of your forbears

Just listen

Routine

By definition it means:
A sequence of actions regularly followed

But for me it's my life
And yeah, I kind of like it that way

Coffee made in the early morning hours just the way I
like it

Soft piano music to go along with the paperwork I'm
pouring over

A predawn walk down a neighborhood street with just
the quiet company of a furry companion

Then the chaos of the morning when my girls awake

Tons of requests
The smell of cocoa and toast as breakfast is made
Of dish soap and laundry as the day begins to purr
along

Then the clamber of chores being done
Vacuums and dust cloths
The doors opening as the puppy runs in and out of the
yard
Her request always at the sound of a small cow bell

The kitten chased up and down and round and round
As the sounds of giggles and calls are heard

We take for granted the sounds of our routines
But I relish them
They are my purpose
And the way I live my life

The breathing coming from a darkened room
Means the night has been well
The request for a missing item
Means the day's tasks are well at hand
And the hundred request that will follow

These are mine to do
And I do so love them
All of them

My routine

Embrace ye thy inner child

Of platinum hair and hazel eyes, she stands beside me
Reaching eagerly for my hand
Her imploring look stirs something deep down inside
I gaze down at her
Feeling lost

You are me? Are you not?
I am she sighs

I am your silly side
The one that plays with stuffed animals and sings songs
all the day through
Who loves the water and the animals

I am your happy side the one that finds joy in
something every single day

I am your compassionate side
That side of you that you give away to those
who needs you

I am your sorrowful side
when the weight of the world is far too much
for even your shoulders

I am your
Adventurous side
Your desire to explore everything around you

To attempt what you may perceive to be impossible
and bring all to its completion

I am all that is you
and sometimes more

I am
That in which you have become
That you are
And always will be

For I am with you

Always

She then squeezed my hand
Smiled up at me
And vanished

I smiled to myself
Knowing that with her
I am never alone
For we are always
there for each other

The eve of the 55th year

You took me into your arms
How I've missed you. I heard you say
I have to tell you how very proud
I am of you
I say that every day

Oh, Daddy I really love you
How I've missed you
and long to talk to you each day
You are always with me in every word I say

I try with all my might I said
to do as you would do
I know, he said and smiled at me
Because I'm watching you

I can see from where I stand each day, he said
I see all of you
I know it's hard but you're doing well and I'm proud of
all of you

You watch us? I asked,
as I looked at him
I do! He smiled again
You see that God Our Father
is my very closest friend

He knew I left you all so fast

and left a void to fill
But you and your dear brother did the job
With such fine skill

So, he lets me watch you every day
But I wanted you to know
that on this day it was special
and I couldn't let it go

So, Happy Birthday Ruska!
My darling daughter dear
This is my gift I give you
And I will always be right here

I woke before the sunrise
A smell of tobacco faintly in the air
For that was a sign to me
Not a dream
but he was there

Winter's icy breath

Winter's icy breath breathes hard against the window
panes
This day as the sun seems reluctant to climb above the
horizon

The glass I gaze out of seems so fragile and delicate on
such a bitter morning
that a mere touch should fracture it and sending its
bone numbing blast in
to chill even my warm and wondering soul

For on this Lovers weekend
I reflect on just what it is
that makes so grand desires of the heart that every
ounce of ones being
be filled to the brim with sheer bliss

Is it the companionship of a lifetime?
That void finally filled

To be content in giving
One must be content in one's self first
Knowing your own heart and mind
To care for the heart that beats so strongly in you
That in turn you can then give without reservation
I sat amongst older couples of evening past and
marveled at the steadfastness

I once wanted that
But am now content with life as I know it
Caring in the way I am for those who love with whole
heart
and have nothing to prove but that their love is the first
love known
and shall be the last love standing in the end

So, as the icy wind of this lover's weekend
Wraps the exterior of our home
It is the Love of a lifetime that keeps its interior safe
warm and protected
This day and many more to come

Peace

Field of clouds

Staring out the window
High above the clouds
I can hear my child's questions
Though it is not mentioned very loud

"Can you see the angels?"

"Is Pop-Pop out there too?"

"Are they safe to walk on?"

"Do I have to wear my shoes?"

I smile at all these questions
for years the answers are always the same

I say, that God has made these fields
for all of us who travel
So that we would surly see

That love ones are always near to us
And angels forever be
Close by our side and watch as we go
From day to day and land to land
From sea to shining sea

So when it is you who travel
And you do so scan the skies

Smile when you see your angel
And wave as you pass by

Milestones

Everyone in their lifetime reaches them
Those achievements that were so long in coming
Those wonderful things that are wanted and waited for
all their lives

Once reached
They are in turn celebrated
Rejoiced upon
And marveled at

Age is one of those milestones
that come to mind today

As loved ones and dear friends mark the passing of
another year
And relish with much forbearance that they themselves
are still amongst those they care so deeply for

We hold our elders fast and with much love and grace
As we celebrate with them
Care for them and marvel at them with as much
conviction as
God Himself must have marveled at his creations

Celebrate with happy heart those of sage wisdom
around you
For theirs is the milestones
We all wish to achieve

Back across the bridge you go

It's your turn you said to the little one
With a twinkle in your eye

It's to her I send you
I can't bear to hear her cry
She so compassionately cared for me
On those long last days
I so long to see her smile again
And see her laugh and play
To take long walks and hear her say
"Oh, how dearly you are loved my sweet little girl
For you make us happier than anything in this world"
She'd say that every day

So, you my little one
go forth and bring delight
Little puppy here you will be missed
But I bid you love and light
And the angels seal it with a kiss
A mark that is for you

Upon your tail she'll see it
For it gleams the purest white
A kiss
A perfect circle
I know they did it right

For you are my gift to her for all years of tender care

For I did so love her
And I watch her there

So, go
play and bring her joy
Make her mad
And bring delight
Let her tell you all her secrets
and stories in the night

Be loyal to the family
who will hold you
greatly in their care
Guard them gently and with love
They'll take you everywhere

So, come my little friend
For its time to go back across that rainbow bridge
It's off to earth you go

So, as the sun did rise that day
an idea and spirit came
to one that was left grieving
And the new soul had passed our way

For you were seen and chosen
And your mark could not be missed
For on your tail you held it
It was that Angel kiss

She knew that you were sent
to her to remember everyday
That Twinkle Twinkle Little Star
Will never fade away

Dragons and Red Wine

Silver rivulets of rain course
down the window pane
Solemn thoughts race about me
as I ponder my place and plain

Down the empty corridors
amidst the many wants
and desires I go
But what lies ahead for me?
One just doesn't know

Where dragons soar above me
My heavy heart made light
It's love that does compel me
Does that somehow make it right?

Weary now from walking
Soon it's time for rest
To allow desire to find me
Peace and happiness

Deep in a glass of red wine
I find my place to hide
Hints of chocolate
and of berries
wish I could reside

So, it is where I delve deep
inside my own recess
to bring out my many memories
and secrets of my success
As the creatures soar above me
and my mind a whirl wind be
it's within the glass before me
that my comfort be

God Feeds the Birds

A simple philosophy really
One I live by day to day
That I believe enriches
The way I make my way

One small token given
Before other demands are said
From my hand to God's creatures
In the form of a slice of bread

Alone on the porch I stand there
tearing into the tiniest of bits
It's food for the wee flyers
You see I can part with this

So, as the good Lord has intended
That we do no harm each day
For He our great provider
And He gently holds us in our stay

He never leaves us hungry
Or wanting for anything
So, I believe I'm honored
To feed those on the wing

So, the rule is simple and
bears repeating now
Prosperity it comes to those who share

As He does feed the creatures of the air
For His never go without
His most tender care

You do for them
He does for you
And He'll Always
See You Through

Lost in the Dark

Miles I seem to walk
A feeling of distance
and foreboding envelopes me

My mind races from one subject
to the next
Stars my lamp light as my universe spins
But I walk on in silence

Years of tarrying on has left a mark
Saddened by the thoughts that age and time were truly
not my greatest ally

Realizing that all the life lessons learned
We're not the kindest

My companion now
the dark and silence of the night
Empty of the clamber
that daylight brings

Conversations of the past at times yield
Painful tear-filled memories

Jaded or bitter was once words used to describe a heart
so broken and so lost
But the outer strength carries forth the deeply broken
and darkened soul

Still I walk on
Though desperate for company once lost
Refuse is taken in the smile of the innocent
The warmth of the furry joviality of a canine or feline
companion
Or the reassurance of the constant of Family and true
friends

Employing as always, a steadfastness
A Champion to all whom are held so dear
It is these darkest hours
That compels me
And aids me
in my own evolution

Mere and brief moments

To be ....

Lost in the Dark

Fireflies dance

A Low-slung moon drifts across the sky
The birds do sing their lullaby
As I sit here
Perchance to see
the fires flies dance
begin for me

In bushes just beyond my walk
I see them there
I shall not talk
I see the swirl and blink
and rise and fall
There special dance to thrill us all

This dance it says that's summers near
Of longer days
And less cares and fears

So, come and raise a glass to them
Our little beacons
Our tiny friends
For they herald in the warm days
of careless fun
And ocean sprays

These little lanterns of delight
They bring us joy and fill our night

So long hail summer
And long hail joy
on tiny wings
They do employ

Left behind

As one deals with all that is the day to day
The thought of being left behind
Is the one at play
today

The madness
The loneliness
That is always at hand
And sadness that holds you
in its very hand

Strength comes in waves you see
As one tends the needs
of the family three
But in the quiet
it's hardly there
As chaos and illness
Take the lion's share

Thoughts that would make
the grown one wail
Swirl about you
like raindrops and hail

You travel and ponder
To set it all right
The sleep when it finds you
comes deep in the night

You know in your heart
the meanings quite true
For you'll rise in the morning
and do what you do

But there is still that feeling
That comes everyday
You've been left behind
To do it this way

If It Be My Will

If it be my will
I would make you
twenty years younger
and pain free
And hear again your laughter
As you stand by me

If it be my will

I'd have you show me more
The ways you used to do things
That way I'd know for sure

If it be my will

No quiet would there be
Of long hours sat in silence
As I'm waiting here
don't you see

If it be my will

Things would be far
different than today
I wouldn't feel so lonely
As I watch you in your stay

But these things are

Not my will

But the ones of God
And it is I who wanders
And solemnly I trod

To do as intended
The way I always do
And silent tears are cried here
These are meant for you

For I cannot fix things
Not all here that is broke
I know every day now
In the hours that you woke

But know that I'm trying
Here with all my might
To make every day a blessing
And somehow keep it right

So, know dear Mom I'll tell you
As I watch from day to day
I will do our family honor
as I proudly make my way

And that be said

It is by my will
and that prophecy
Be true

Summer storms

Just five more minutes
As sleep tossed
I snuggle deeper into my pillow

Then a lighting flash
And a crack of thunder
I rise to view a cloud filled sky
Black and foreboding
Lighting dancing in deliberate streaks

Then comes the rain
In a torrent
Curtains of cool relief
Sending drop to glide down the window panes

The foliage seems to reach for it nourishing touch as
the drops glisten on each and every leaf

The pitter-pat a melody played on the sidewalk
The driveway shines in the lamplight as if it had been
freshly painted

The world washed anew

Blessed be
thy summers storm

Jewels in the Garden

While engrossed in my chores today
I spied a flash as it flew my way
A tiny streak of yellow I see
Among the flowers
not far from me

I see you dart from stem to stem
Around the way
And back again

Atop a flower you gently perch
Another morsel
that is, you're search
And as I gentle turn away
You're gone again
And on your way

Then as if by magic
A friend I see
Amongst the flowers
just feet from me

Tiny wings to carry right
Amongst the flowers
held in thy sight

For you are a tiny treasure flying there
Your brilliant colors are meant to share

You dash and dart
and hover so
And bring me joy
I hope you know

That little birdies
Flying there
Fill me with glee
Your beauty rare
what joy you bring
This very day
I pray with love
And hope you stay

Cricket's Serenade

In the corners
I hear their song
Soft and sweet
and all night long

Their tiny chirping
fills the night
As stars come out
to show their light

As if to call
it's the end of day
No more work
or time to play

For its time to dream
a dream they say
And sigh a sigh
Till the break of day

For we shall lull you
That we'll try
To easy you
with a lullaby

So, listen quietly
all through the night
each tiny note

performed just right
As cricket's songs
do tend to fade
So, listen to
their serenade

Solace

Consoled only by the household hum
I revel in the quiet
before the chaos comes
On cat like feet I do the things
I know that must be done
And I do them all in silence
before the rising sun

Of meds and chores
I start my day
Long ahead of plan
This my only time alone
I take it when I can

Coffee made and laundry
Animals all fed too
Then it's off to my cozy chair
For a brief moment or two

For then the whirlwind starts
As the house begins to stir
Of footsteps and closing doors
and walkers in the hall

Soon the requests are fast coming
As they often do
Of all manner of things wanted
"Mom, I can't find my shoe!"

So, my time is broken
as I put quiet thoughts away
And head off to care for others

For its just another day

Fifty four years my friend you be

I do so Love you
yes, I do

from one that Loved us
we now are Two

Forever playmates to rule the day
Forever friends the way we'll stay

to teach
to share
to love
to care

to follow each other
everywhere

A birthday wish I give to you
that is our bound
forever true

that you will be my guiding star
I love to watch you going far

Burn bright and shine on in the night
you lead our Family
and do it right

so Happy Birthday brother dear

and know forever

I'm glad your near

Confusion

Confused am I as time
passes so slowly

Confused am I that
I know not all that
is placed before me

As my day to day walk
Is mired by these thoughts
The path both long and lonely

From sunrise to sunset as I toil
I pray that I serve all with love and faith
Honesty and knowledge in my heart to give and care
for all of my days

I see with my eyes
the failing of my heart
As age lays waste
to the body of the one who
held me all of my days

I shall give to thee
my heart and soul
My strength in these last days

I shall sing of the joys
that we have shared

over all these years
For we shall never
pass this way

Again

Time changes all

The thrum of rain beats steadily
As old friends meet today
With joy they greet each other
For its just another day

But time has made each different
One jovial and so gay
The other one is guarded
and a bit distant
But together they do stay

The ones who care sit watching
As the two talk into the night
Enjoying their new friendship
Each one differs in their plight

Why is time a taker
Of those we know and love?
Why are those who care left wanting
Feeling like we have just been shoved?

For change it comes to taunt us
And time it is a thief
For we too shall see it
As if beyond belief

To take from us the things we love
The ones we hold so dear

And changes us all forever

And leave us standing here

So, I say you today
Give warmly and with care
For each day is a gift given
And it so very meant to share

Revival in each tiny joy
No matters just how small
For it is time that shall change it
And change it one and
All

Lost in Autumn's Rain

The wind sings and rustles the leaves outside my
window
The ones fallen
like puppies bounding
about my feet
Skittering across the lawn
Playfully teasing my imagination
With tales they are so ready to tell

I lose myself to the playful energy that surrounds me
And cherish the boundless excitement that with each
new tale
my Autumn casts her spell

Leading me in new directions
Filling me with love and awe
She is forever by me
I see things I have never saw

So, come and listen to
these tales I tell you
To make you happy
bright and gay

As a small soul will fill you
and send you on your way

Season of Thanksgiving

Frost covers all things this day
As dawn it softly breaks
A falcon softly takes its perch
To spy a meal to take

I wonder as I mostly do
What makes the leaves to fall?
For in this time of year I see
it's time to share with all

This season is upon us
To give with a grateful heart
As love ones gather near us
In this season we impart

A sense of love and sharing
These things we wish to give
Of self and joy and happiness
In ourselves and where we live

Time tested recipes
Mixed with love and care
These are the things we give each other
in this season of love and care

So, gather one and all I say
To give thanks to the Lord above

For if nothing else these days
we have each other's love

A Week Before Christmas

It's the week before Christmas
And all through my house
not a sound can be heard here
from a dog or a mouse

The girls are still sleeping all warm in their beds
One dreaming of Santa that can safely be said

The presents are ready to go on their way
It's a matter of days now to give them away

The cookies are baked and the tree is all trimmed
And we are all ready
for a visit from
Him

In the still of the morning with coffee in hand
I am ready for Christmas
oh, this year I am

To enjoy the peace that this season does bring
And the laughter and visits and that sort of thing

For the one thing I wanted to have most of all
Has come to pass
Was good health to my family and peace to us all

So, as this week finishes

I say to you

Merry Christmas my friends
And God Bless us too

Was asked of late

"Does Liz still believe in Santa Clause?"
"Oh yes, yes she does!" Was my reply.

As I reflect on that question as I walk the dog down the darkened street
In the glow of the neighborhood Christmas decorations

I ponder why is it we all don't still believe?

Walking through the Mall just yesterday it saddened me to think that

Life has gotten so busy and so detached from one another the we fail to believe in anything

Alone Santa sat on his throne

Waiting

To hear those deeply held desires
Of our innocence
Those guarded desires that are meant for just one person to hear

But we have lots of people who hear us these days

But are they listening?

To not just the words but the heartfelt desire of our
bygone youth

Are they hearing with an open heart and mind?

As Santa leaned in to hear my child's innocent
Requests

He was thoughtful and caring
And for a brief moment
I heard again that sleigh bell
Faintly ringing in my own Christmas past

And I know in my heart of hearts
Christmas is kept and
kept well within me

As I try to give hearts desire
To bring some joy to each day
To make merry in my own rite and way
And to carry on as God has truly intended

That was all that Christmas was and is supposed to be

So how do you keep yours?

Winter Windsong

Her tune it rises sweetly
Lifting slowly in the night
Against a star filled backdrop
And drifting out of sight

It's carried to the heavens
To have the angels hear
The song that the wind does sing
Is ringing soft and clear

I stand in utter silence
And listen with all my might
to those voices that are singing the voices of the night
The ones that sing of beauty as they play on before first
light

Surrounded by their ringing
And steadfast in their sound
Their tone it sends me reeling
As my spirit leaves the ground

For they carry me with them

These rising ringing tones

For I am so inspired
and not so all
Alone

So, as winter fast approaches

and stars still fill the skies

I will always listen
As the wind sings
her lullabies

For Thee I sing

Through the very air I fly
As if on eagles' wings
Across thy purple majesty
It is for thee I sing

I so wish we stood together
One nation and one land
To walk and talk as brothers
And proudly we would stand

But times they are trying
And tensions they run high
And I do say a prayer today
As I ride across the sky

That we will know compassion
And we shall all be blessed
By the One who knows
what's in our heart
and bids us do our best

So, it is a blessing for the New Year
That we lay the past aside
Remember Peace and understanding
in our hearts it shall abide

So, lay aside the hardships
and thy furrowed brow

And know we shall get through this
Our Maker will show us how

So, the happiest of New Years
Is what bid to you
As our adventures will now unfold

For the past it is behind us
They're now tales
that will be told

Happy 2019

Dixie Raindrop

A soft and steady rainfall
Is thrumming overhead
As safely in our cabin
the ones I love are cuddled in their bed

As raindrops tap the tin roof
and a fire softly glows
A sense of peace surrounds me
As so this story goes

I go out on the front porch
To contemplates and pray
That today it will be better
Then all my yesterdays

There are ducks out on the river
For I can hear them call
And the rivers running faster
I can see it trip and fall

It a little slice of heaven
Though under cloudy skies
Is what we have in Dixie
and it comes as no surprise

For like those all around me
Who come from far and near
It is the peace that are these mountains

And I know they're glad
They're here

So, listen to songs that sing
From nature and your heart
And you will remain here
In Dixie's steadfast heart

On the riverside

There she stands my refuse
The place I will abide
She's standing there waiting
Along the riverside

Of roughhewn timbers she is made
With a porch that calls come sit
And tell of your adventures or just come rock a bit

Inside there are all manner of
Creature comforts there
A tiny living room with a sofa and a chair
There's a little tiny kitchen just big enough for three

It just perfection here
It's perfect for me
you see

There is one more thing that delights me
As I set upon my gaze
is the fireplace before me
as I watch its dancing blaze

You see I've fallen in love here with people and the land
But I'm sorry to say
I have to go

My leaving is at hand

But one day I will come back here
And roam the mountains high
Because I do so love it here

Where Blue smoke fills the sky

Tear drops and snowflakes

Crystal flakes of white dance in the glow of the
streetlamp

As an old heart beats on in the dark

Years of emotions stream into old hands
In the wee small hours as a mother and child hold fast
to all that they are to one another

A world of lament is at last laid out
And all the is held is cast into the darkness
As the embrace is deepened

Wondering if there is more of this world that can or
shall be done

It is this broken heart

That has seen the pain
Shared the joys
Endured the miles of experiences that have truly
Made a life

But now amidst and among the deepening black of
these wee small hours and the
Icy breath of winter

I feel not the kiss of these tiny snowflakes

But the bite of the frosty air as time's dance begins to
slow

She my dear one the only friend of a lifetime

knows me

Now it is I that must be strong
So, as snowflakes dance in the lamplight
And memories of an age go swiftly into these wee small

I shall be what the Maker has intended

Steadfast for home and hearth
Brave for those who cannot
Compassionate of those whose intentions are well
meant
And patient of all others

Though it be said I am
Not patient now or of late
But this too shall be learned

So, swirl on
Tiny flakes of snow for this night
is now and forever shall be cast in the memories of a
house that love has truly built
For one who had given love and life to us all here

Mommy

Alone

In a word it conjures an image of
Solitude

For me is it the feeling
I've carried for years

Thought it be a
filmy misty shroud that surrounds
me in my quietest moments
Or should I speak of the
Loss of self on that which is
of its most hectic days

It is always with me
As life's lessons present themselves
Time and time again
Day after day

It is the aloneness that is what has become my
companion

Pulling me to her
She wraps me in her embrace and
And penetrates my soul

As if she is me
and I become like the air
Just breath that is so essential

But nothing more
than breath

As I rise
she greets me
As I travel
she goes too

In the quiet of the dawn
or the stillness of a sunset
She clasps my hand
and is there

Her misty sad eyes haunt me
Filling me with the tears of a thousand broken promises
and a million lost days

Try as I might
Wanting as I do
I wish she would leave me

The embrace of joy that would be unending but even
though there is joy
She stands there
Alongside me

The emptying feeling at the end of the day
that is all that I have truly become

As the house quiets
And the silence surrounds me she is there

Her hands out stretched to embrace me once more

You are mine
And I am you
she whispers

For this is what you have
created
Your world
And I shall be forever with you

Alone

First to change

You have a child
Ten fingers ten toes
A healthy cry
The story goes

As time goes by
You see a change
A gesture
A whine
Something seems strange

You're busy and stressed
You're all on your own
Only the help of
your family nearby
They're there for you always
with each tear you cry

Then comes that one day
You hope as you seek medical care
Your fears won't be realized
With hope
do you dare

But news is a hard one
On the day of your birth
Came the news that you dreaded
It did shake the earth

At age twenty-nine
Autism reared its head
It grabbed hold of your child
And filled you with dread

Where do we go?
How will we get by?
To find help you go
You sought out the wise

Remember what you were taught!
Came that voice
These her wise words
Your banner or curse
But to this malady
you were given
No choice

Away through your days
You gave it your all
This strange thing called autism
Would not beat us all

Your daughter grew stronger
With each passing day
And you were her teacher
She would not slip away

From program to program
You'd try anything
For she was your child and

She made your heart sing

As the years became shorter
And lessons she'd learn
 it was for a bright future
Your heart it did yearn

She did to the wonder of
family and friend
She finished her schooling
But this is not the end

She is a marvel
This daughter of yours
As she goes day by day
Happily doing her chores

You have given her purpose
And travel and fun
As she stands there beside you
in the glow of the sun

Autism
Has come to this family you see
It did give our lives meaning
Not just an existence to be

So, if this thing
That is autism comes
and pays you a call

I say rise to the challenge
And embrace it
All

Round and Round

It's there with you as you travel
It will not set you free
That feeling that does follow
That won't ever let you be

It's that inner voice
I'm hearing
The one that speaks to me

I hear it almost daily
That whisper in my ear
"Do you know what you are doing?
Do you know just why you're here?"

You are your Father's daughter
Caring, strong and wise
But sometimes you falter
That comes as no surprise

You put others far before yourself
As true as the sun does rise
Being for them the leader
A trait cherished
and so prized

But when the night comes
So does sadness
At times lonely and a bit blue

It's that want of company
that no one really does understand

just you

Pushing that down deeper
So, no one knows it's there
A smile
a nod
and it's gone from them
This is your fare facade

You wonder if they care

You're out to keep them guessing
Guarding who it is you'll be
As you travel day to day
Be just the way you are now
That person they like to see

But inside you know the heartache
The troubles and the fears
Alas you're only human
There's no harm in showing tears

So, it's round and round
This dance is done
It goes on and on
My friend
I think is the one I'll do
For now, until my end

Pictures of home

The sun slowly creeps over the horizon on this lovely
summer's day
As I quietly make my way back home
Nary do I stray

Back inside I go about
And tend some small chores
As I slowly begin a day
where nothing is quite sure

Inside the house is quiet
Fans tuning silently overhead
While the ones I cherish are sleeping in their beds
Beams of sunlight through the curtains cast patterns on
the rug
My family is still off dreaming cuddled up like little
bugs

Me I set about the house
Starting supper and some things
Darting here and there
as if on hummingbird wings

Around me are my treasures
Trinkets from here and there
Photo and great memories of
all the times that we do share

Forty-six years we've been here
This our castle and our home
Through good times and in sorrow
We all can find our comfort
And never truly roam

Bought by a simple couple
To raise their family strong
To give a place for roots
Somewhere where they belong

Inside is quite modest
Filled with love and many joys
Upstairs you may find a room
With far too many toys

But aside from all the things here
There is one that stands fast
It's the love that built this home
And live is meant to last

So, from my rocker on the porch
I sing this simple song
Be ever so humble
There's no place quite like home

Precious in thy sight

To behold you as I do
and hold you near
and dear to me

For the wonderment of you
is all I need to see

But as age comes to these eyes
and may one day begin to fade
I hold thee precious in thy sight
forever and a day

For I have beheld miracles
Of the birth of my only child
I too have seen wonders
as I've traveled many miles

I've embraced the happiness
of loves youthful glow
And held hands with loneliness
as I watched matrimonial love go

I've seen through these eyes
The miracle of life
And watched life fade away
with little pain and strife

I'm sad as I begin to think

The curtain shall grow
dark

But I figure hell
It's never been
a walk about the park

I stand as this is given me
a new pain for to deal
But I do understand it
And I'll willing take the wheel

This challenge will not beat me
As I head long into it
Blindness does not frighten me
It's mine each little bit

So, one day
when the shadows fall
I will not cry out in despair
For I have beheld you all
And hold you precious in thy sight
Every tiny moment
And that somehow makes it right

So, if this all sound foolish
or a little off to you
I say this to all who read this

What is it
you would do?

Winter Garden

From the terrace I can see
A beautiful gold finch
he sings for me

As he darts from tree to tree
His song so shrill
and sweet it be

Under a gray and sunless sky
I watch with joy
as he flies by

And it is with this
I am reassured
That this winter weather
Shall be endured
For only a very few weeks more

I long for days of the sun to shine
and while away the hours thine

So, sing on my gentle little friend
For soon the winter
it shall end

And you will call to this heart of mine

Come out to play

for now,
it is time

Spring is here to stay you see
That you will
gladly say to me

As your friends happily appear
and they will stay in the garden here
for you are happy
Bright and gay
I love the fact
that you are here to stay

Oh, what a merry sight to see
The birds returned and rejoicing
In the trees

To fill our garden
Here with song

I could listen to them
all day long

So, come and join me if you will
for in our garden you too can fill
the air so sweetly with your songs
So, we can listen all winter long

To the horizon

I walked along your icy shore
My soul longing for sea
Across the distant horizon
The siren sings to me

No matter what the season
I can hear her distant song
It can wake me from my slumber
Or can haunt me all day long

Her voice it's like the crashing
of the waves upon shore
It resonates within me
down to my very core

Until I cannot bare it
She calls to me
once more

Come to me
I'm waiting
The voice rises from the sea
For I have so missed you
The siren sings to me

So, I cast away my worries and my cares for all that day
to stand along the water's edge
So, I can hear her say

You have come to see me
Oh, what joy
Is what I hear her say

For it has been too long now please don't go away

I smile as the icy spray
kisses my chilly cheeks
And sea birds dance above the foamy swells that rise
in mounting peaks

I'm here I say to the siren
The one that fills my soul
With such joy
and such devotion
She takes a steadfast role

On taming my emotions
But not leading me astray
Just teaching me her lesson
So, can I go on each day

So, if a siren sings to you
And you'll know it
if she should

Heed her call
For she knows
it is all for
your own good

What comes next?

It's this question that puzzles me
as I sit and think each day you see
For so many things are in my care

And I shall take them anywhere

but at times

the roads are not so smooth
and it is I alone that stands to lose
the ways that I have always known
for one day the kingdom will be dethroned

and maybe if you look closely, you'll see
the tear and things that worry me

the care and love that I so give
that all around me shall happily live

with the worry and the strife
that fills
this not so ordinary life

Of beast and kin so rightly be
and tend their lives so joyously

Of sickness and of maladies
tis I their comforts

that are sought from me

But it's I whose worry is there each day
In lines that are drawn and hair of gray

To go on attending as I do
And no complaints
I say to you

Care as well as well can be

For God looks on
and smiles at thee

For these are good works
He sees me do
As from day to day
I see it through

But as I do
I wonder so
Is this my way
I need to go

Sometimes so lonely this road be and as I do
I wish to see
A hand of help extends to me
It comes some days
from nurses' fair
who shares the load

The ones I bare

Who come with sound advice to give
To shed some light on this life I live

From stories to remedies
that they know
Impart their knowledge
then they go

But back into the quiet see
After the teaching

it's just me

To do as I always do
With gentle hands and a tear or two

The ones I love will always be
first in my heart
With care from me

So, if you see with your own eyes
Some days are gray
It's no surprise
That I am here
for them
I hope you see

And come awhile
and sit with me

For each day that question
is still waiting there

What comes next?

And

Will you be There?

I Shall Rise

There will come a day
that You will call me

On a gentle breeze
I shall rise

On wings of color
I shall rise

On the softest strains of sweet music
I shall rise

So, cry not
Grieve not

For
I shall rise

To walk with the most High
And be surrounded by those
I Have loved

And who have loved
Me

I shall rise

And I am

Free

Amen

Missing you

I awoke from a dream
Walked into your room
You were there resting
But then again soon

The sun will come
find the way that you are
But your past is behind you
and that's not there
where you are

I long for your stories
The ones of just we
You would repeat them
over and over
You'd say them all to me

I sit by your bedside
And watch day by day
As time takes your memories
And goes slipping away

I long as your daughter
The strength and the pride
To do things together
And stand side by side

But time is a thief

That steals you from me
It takes hold your health
and binds you

You see

I wonder what God thinks
as we travel each day
Is He guiding my steps?

Is he hold you closer?
till you fade away?

I don't really bother with
others these days
My focus surrounds you
So, it here you will stay

Mama I'm lonely
As lonely can be
And when I see you hurting

It's slowly destroying me

But I gather my courage
And go forward each day
Our family together

The way it should stay

I wish beyond reason

To turn back the time
But I know in that ability

I know it's not mine

So, as time move on forward
As it always does
I'm here to love you
I do this because

I am your daughter
And here come what may

I'll stand by you forever
I know
it's the way

But it's true
I still miss you
our days in the sun
For you're a great teacher

And I am the one
Who has learned a great deal
From the preaching you did

And it's of these
Old and fines lessons that I go
On to live

The life that you gave me

And oh, come what may

I'll stand by you forever

Forever to stay

Daybreaks

Gales blow across the open sky
Makes the clouds of white
go sailing by
Like ships upon the ocean do
My spirit has been set anew

The hues they are
aplenty see
Of pinks and blues
and peach
It be

It's fairy floss in the sky today
It makes my heart feel
light and gay

I feel my heart has been lifted
I feel brighter than before
That I can now do
even more today
Then have ever done before

The darkness it has abated
The shadows are no more
And brightness it surrounds me
Like the waves along the shore

I stride through my day to day

Without a single care
To do what is before me
Work without the ware

Merrily the tasks complete
As one by one they go
Till day is done
And with reverence
all I have to show

A happy fulfilled household
A happy family they be
Even our beloved pet
all tended to you see

For today it is blessing
To rise and feel renewed
No dark clouds on the horizon
Just clear skies
to see me through

Those Days

There are those days
When cascading sheets of rain
is all you see and feel

Your soul so dark and heavy
That even the daybreak
leaves nary a glimmer of hope for you

Then there are those day
That hope lays in great abundance
Your heart is light
and all is right in your world

I cast my eyes on both of these
Lost and abandoned one day
 jubilant the next

But of all of these days
I say this one way or another
It is truly is a blessing
That God has
Blessed and surrounded me
with the grace and strength
He knows what
he has designed me for

Though I don't always agree
With these plans

I will see them all through

As maddening or joyous

These are
those days
That God has made for
Me

And I shall be gracious
For Those Days

Amen

Lessons

Take heed to that's all around you
For there are lessons to be learned

Of times when life's a teacher
And it's for your mind to earn

Take heed to wind and water
To the birds and beasts that are there

For to you they shall impart
Their wisdom
For they have many stories to share

Take heed to those who befriend you
For not only companions they be
They to shall be your teachers
And instruct you to see differently

Life it is a classroom
we enter the day we are born
Each moment alive is a lesson
Of this
I am totally sworn
For we shall never stop learning

As we go on day by day

The Great Spirit that is our teacher
has designed it
to be taught just that way

All in a day's work

Arising early everyday

To get my things done
this I say

It comes as no surprise to me
The things that are done
for my family three

The chores the stores and paperwork
To toil and tarry and run-about

It's all that done with love and caring be
For those who make up my family three

Our fur babies are here as well
To cheer our hearts
and with tales to tell

A canine fair as fair can be
A feline playing happily
Of reddish coat they both are
With shining eyes much like the stars
They bring this family joy you see
And fill our home with wanted glee

As sunshine marks the day begin
I know that I am off again

To do the bidding of my little clan

As God abides and I understand
It's not a lot I have you see
But this is my lot in life for me

Swimming Free

Little fishy swimming there
Around and round without a care
As you are here to bring a smile
I hope with love
you stay awhile

A flash of blue and white I see
As you go by
then look at me

Serenity is in your wake
as loving eyes will
behold and take
A joy that she alone will see
A fishy swimming happily

You're as beautiful
as all our pets
I smile and think
I'm glad we met

So, sitting here and watching you
Oh, our dear Stitch
I say this true
I'm glad you're here
to warm our hearts

And bring a smile
that you impart

Like moving tie-dye in a bowl
You'll be loved
and have some small control
To hold attention
and soothe a soul

So little fish of blue hues
I say with heart
we love you true

Momma's Prayer

I overheard this morning
And it came as no surprise

The prayers of my dear sweet
Momma

And it brought tear to these old eyes

I heard her words of
Love and Thanksgiving

And I also heard her say

That she
herself was happy

And that she felt
well today

She asked God for continued blessings
to fall upon
each of her family dear

I heard her speak of the angels
To have them gather around us and stay
and keep us all from fear

I smiled to myself at this vision

As it made my heart
so light and gay

For all that she has been through
And whatever may come her way

I know my momma is grateful
It's in her prayers each day

I am confident in saying

That I know

God does listen
To all she has to say

But

it's I

Who loves to listen to

My Momma's Prayers

Each day

When I am free

When I am free
I will walk in the light and not be afraid

When I am free
I will spend a little time and just think of me
When I am free

I will play in the sun with nary a care
And I may just go anywhere

When I am free

My child will see
a truly different side of me

But today is
not that day you see

I am duty bound and worried be

My elder she my charge be
To be loved and cared for so you see

I gaze into those now vacant eyes
that once beheld
and blazed with light

A distance is now in its place
as I look upon her ancient face

Sorrow she walks by my side

The tears I shed at night are cried

For no one is allowed to see
The heartache here
inside of me

I seek God's comfort as I go
And know He sees my tears of woe

Stay calm and clear
with each passing day
for I am with you
along this way

My angels
I send to thee
So, you are not alone
you see

Carry on daughter
Continue to fight
for I am with you
in your plight

And one day
Your toiling will end
you see

It all shall cease

You'll be set free

For you have a great task there
And soon repose will be your share

Have faith
Be kind
And stay your path

For freedom is:

your

Aftermath

Take thee into thy arms

I said to my self

What is my faith

I have the faith
that the Lord watches
over me and mine

I have faith
in all who give of their hearts

I have faith that God
in all of His power and wisdom

Holds those whom I have ever loved
close and protects them

I place these of all things into His arms

But mostly I put my mother
In to Thy arms
For she has fought long and hard
to be the person who

Molded her children

Stood gallantly beside the husband
that she loved with all her heart

Rose above the challenges of her life
To become her children's hero

So, with that

I humbly ask

Take thee into Thy loving arms

Oh Lord

The one I love with my whole heart

For she does live and worship
As a true servant

And is deservingly worthy of
all Your love and grace

Amen

Light side of Dark Days

In a room
Where little hope
is shared
a ray of faith
to me is spared

I say the things
I feel are true

And everyday
I search for You

With company
of those who care
And it's in their healing
hands they share

To guild
And teach
And tell their tales
And through their works
They do not fail

I listen to the words they say
And with open mind
I make my way

Into the darkness

I do go

At times it really
scares me so

But I sally forth

Though I be afraid
of this unknown
I know inside
I'm not alone

For it's with a grateful heart
I say this true

If prayers are said
He walks you

Into the darkness
You may head
And in your heart
you're full of dread

With tender heart
He hears your strife
From heaven's edge
He sees your life

His intervention
is swift and true
It's how he shows

His Love for you

To show you

You are not alone

So, go bravely
Protect your own

And return the love
He gives to you

For true miracles
Can come your way

I say this true

I did today

May God Be Praised

Come Sunday

Under gray skies and raindrops
She enters

Walking ever so lightly as she goes

You rise
Feeling her near
and embracing arms

Her touch as soft as angels wing

And you smile
For it truly a new day

Inside resides a sense of peace

Long missed

But now there

You walk to the window
Watching the raindrops trace their way down the glass
and breathe a sigh

Peacefully you make your way into the day

Awake and aware
Strength regained

and purpose
Renewed

Task are done with joy
And
Praise be given
to the Most High

For with this Devine intervention
And this sense
that seems to have no merit

So, I say
Come Sunday
Bring your peace
Your joy
And your love
For this we shall do for all of
His grace

Amen

My Father's Robe

Rising early this I say
I was missing so
my Dad today

So, from my slumber
I did rise
And sought his robe
It's not my size

But in its worn and softness there
I feel his arms and tender care

I've kept it
for the summer days
To recall with love
his meandering ways

When summer fun
will call to me
and in the sun
we will all be

But mostly I don this robe
to remind me of
my days of old

When he stood by me
day by day

and taught me lessons
along the way

His stories and tales
of things he did
and the trouble he got into
as a kid

But mostly I hear him
in these
Lost days

I Love you,
Ruska!
I'd hear him say

For that was his pet name for me
As he would guild me knowingly

For its in his robe
that I now wear
And gather courage that
we both shared

I carry on from day to day
But know he's with me
along the way

I know he's proud of
the way I go
Caring, loving

this I know

So, I realize
I'm not in fashion see

But in his robe
He's close by me
As I go along
from chore
To chore

I'm wrapped in love

Of this I'm sure

If tattered and old this robe be

It's

My Father's robe

That covers me

Today's Artwork

Come draw me a picture
Come paint me a smile

Come my dear child
entertain me awhile

As the day ticks away
And the tasks are complete

I'm in need of your joy
To make the toiling
seem fleet

With pencils and crayons
Pastels and paint

I'm in love with your creations
Each one is so quaint

So, bring me your magic
on this rainy day
For well shall have rainbows
And dragons today

Timeless

I was thinking of late
of my life thus far

Who would have thought
I'd have come so far

A mother
a daughter
A caretaker me

As I tend to my family
each day

You see

But I can't help but think
of my friends all around

As time marches forward
With nary a sound

From honors bestowed
for good grades
they have earned

And graduation
for all of the lessons
that they have well

Learned

I watch with wide wonder
The passing of time

As new children are add
to extend
My friends line

But here it is different
as different
can be
For path here

is timeless

For my young one and me

The day may seem ordinary
To ones who don't know
But we keep moving forward
in our way that we go

The likes of mother are the same
For her child
And we do as we do
with so much as a smile

It's colors and music
Animation and rest
And

Edible treats
that we love the best

So, as we go together
my child and me
Our dance on this earth
Is timeless you see

For she be my dragon
And I her unicorn
And we are together
Our alliance is sworn

For we two
Are timeless

As these beasts of old
And together forever
Our tales will be told

For we have each other
And like it this way

We are both
Timeless
And that way
we will stay

Maybe

Maybe you'll find peace
in knowing you were there
When the need
was the greatest

Maybe you'll see
all the action
Took place for
the family's
Greater good

Maybe you'll realize
That it took
The Lion and the scorpion
Standing side by side
To vanquish an enemy
we could not defeat alone

Maybe you'll find peace
In knowing
you will never be alone

Or

Maybe

you'll just find

Peace

As it is

In the all mighty stillness
One thought seems to resound
I have given all I could
And in that
all love
does abound

As family strength is measured
In heartbeats here today
We stand steady and united
As Darkness heads our way

Each of us share this nightmare
And we handle it our own way
But we love and guild each other
As we head into the fray

For what may come
will be a battle

A struggle of the heart

But that
that does not kill us
Will make us stronger
But it will never
tear us apart

So, I sit and give to my God
All my worries and my tears
And He sees what he does see
My deep cares and all my fears

But I realize that today is fate

For He knows in all His wisdom
And that's far more than me
So, I close eyes and open my heart
And into God's hand lay my strife

For I know the we're all
Praying for the continuation of life

Another Sunrise

Another sunrise
Another new day
To keep us together
Amidst of the fray

I stand here and bask
In dawns golden glow
And know in my heart
that we've so far to go

The sea bird goes winging
Out over the waves
And we have in ourselves
Our ways to be brave

For the trials they were many
As the month it did pass
But we knew of these things
That they too
would not last

So away we did journey
To stand on the shore
Surrounded in glory
And to hear waves lore

So, I say to you
When trials abound

Come listen in earnest
To nature's sweet sound

For nothing is promised
And nothing may stay

But it is this
that is given

Another Sunrise

Today

Gray Lullaby

Amongst the towering white caps
And the thrumming of the rain
The gulls are loudly calling
I hear their shrill refrain

The beach is now abandoned
As all now head inside
No one's out walking
For now, it is high tide

A brisk and damp winds blowing
As flags billow in the air
And raindrops sting your skin
As their falling without care

It's amusing as the weather
Can turn greatly at its will
And if one is not so careful
one might dare to catch a chill

But within the walls of comfort
Lounging in repose
The ones I love do slumber on
And happily, they doze

So, under steel skies I sit
As sea birds swirl near by
Staring out at the cool gray water

With nary a teardrop in my eye

I know that I am lucky
As lucky as can be
For no matter
the temperament of weather
My family's here with me

So, in the still sweet silence
Underneath a steel gray sky
The wind and sea
still sing to me

It's restless lullaby

The memory thief

A crime has happened here today
It came and stole my friend away

It tip-toed in without a sound and
Left me here with no rebound

The one it touched
has changed you see

She stares and is lost
as lost can be

Her mind a jumble of all she knew
She speaks as well
alas that's true
The tales she tells go round and round
And make no sense

But do resound

Of memories that once were there
But now untruths are dwelling there

Where is the Mom
that loved me so
I want her back!
Where did she go?

The one that's living
now in her place
She stares at me
and knows still my face

But her words confused
Her tales seem odd

I cry inside

Oh no dear God

Please not now
Please give to me
the Mom that
raised me lovingly

But in the fray, it walked today
The memory thief
And stole my Mom away

A tangle of words
it left in its wake
I'm heartbroken and lonely
and all for whose sake

She will not be left for others to care
For she is my mother and no burden to share

I wonder as I see her today
Will she still remember?

Will she be ok?

The ones who are caring for her
Seem to know
As I ask directions
on which way to go

They say to go lightly
and go with great care
And to keep loving
Let her know
you are there

Keep your hands soft
as you toil everyday
And she may stay with you
along this long way

There are many reasons
The thief comes to call
But
You must remember
There's no fault at all

Sometimes it just happens
to the ones that we love
And pray now for guidance
Rain help from above

Beware I'm am telling
to ones who will read

Of thieves that come calling
and
Memories they'll bleed
Away from the ones
who gave you
your life

Sometimes they come slowly
Sometimes not at all

But if they come swiftly
Your heart takes the fall

So please heed my warning

I say this is true

The memory thief is out there

It can happen to you

Summer sounds

The quiet whirring of the fan
Slowly turning above my head

The peaceful sounds of slumber
As loved ones lay in bed

The chirping of the birds outside as they do start to call

These are the sounds of summer
I love listening to them all

The lapping of the waves I hear
As the water meets the shore
The sea birds cry and carry on
A meal for them I'm sure

The restlessness of the ocean seems to mirror the way I
feel
As I stand upon the sand
My thoughts begin to reel

For summer it has changed for me as I tell you here
today

The sounds that still call to me
Will never go away

It's peace and calm and

Wanderlust

That bids me come and play

And set aside the stresses
That does carry you away

I let the sounds surround me
As often as I can

And dream of distant islands
and standing on the sand

So, I say to this season
Do listen with all your heart

Because summer is so fleeting
And soon school bells
they will start

Take comfort

Take comfort in knowing
that I will always be here
Surrounding you with all the things
that you yourself hold dear

Take comfort in the knowledge
that no one will do you harm
No strange hands will tend you
As you slowly go along

Take comfort in
the love that's here
Unending day to day
By the family that loves you
as the years does slip away

Take comfort if you will today
That your legacy will survive
For the ones that you have reared so well
Will stand steadfast by your side

Take comfort as you rest your head
Your precious shall endure
A life that is overseen by
faith and love
and happiness for sure

These are the things I promise
My troth
I give to thee

Take comfort that no matter
What
you've heard this straight from me

Star-spangled wonderment

The sky is alight with the fire of twelve million stars
As I sit enveloped in a cloak of ebony silence

Within this realm of possibilities
I alone
ponder the wisdom of
The Most High

Where is the justice in this life?
that is poured out before me
each and every day

Why I wonder
Are the things that I experience
So difficult to manage and understand

That with the knowledge that I was granted
The mere comprehension leaves me so drained and
distraught

Days fall like leaves now
one after another
I await a time that a great gail will cast these aloft
Swirling about me
setting my very soul
free once more

But for now, I am bound fast

To all that is in my charge

Guiding, nurturing
Those around me

But I do so wish
That good health was theirs
Soundness of mind
and spirit were theirs

These are the things I would desire for those in my care
and who have my heart each day

So if my sense of wonderment would ever be addressed
By our Lord
These are the things
I would wish to know

And I know
I would
really
listen

Mirror images

In my youth I was given a task
To stand before the looking glass
My council had instructed me
To take mental note
of the one I see

Do this alone
it was said to me
And see the person
you are meant to be

So, days later
I did as I was told
I disrobed and stood there

Young and bold

To see the youth
that God graced me
My eighteen years
for me to see

Perhaps a bit thinner
I thought aloud
as I turned and gazed
And feeling quite proud

Not at all shy

of girl before me
Who's image in glass
smiled back at me

I recall dressing
and feeling quite sure
of the things that I knew
and how they would
endure

I've repeated this exercise
Many times, through the years
And I stood and I marveled
at the fact
that I'm still here

Though the outsides changed
And the head has grown wise
I know that the heart
is the one thing that I prize

For the image that now
I see in the glass
Has learned to take pleasure
from things of the past

The lessons I've learned from those all around
Have molded and shaped me and still they astound

So now in my fifty's
I stand here today

Well gifted with treasures
they can't take away

Silver now glints in my tresses
You see
And maybe not as toned
as I once was
you see

But I've fallen in love
With the me
that resides
Down deep in my soul
and I say this with pride

If I were to pass
this lesson to you
Would you see your image?
The one that is true?

Would it give you pleasure?
Down deep from within
Or would you long to return
To where you begin

So, this is a challenge
I give unto you

Seek the mirrors image and see

If it's True

Don't wish them away

The days
they get long
And frustrating at times
But don't wish them away
The ones that are thine

For they did stand nearest
to you everyday
And they listened and worried
And cared in their way

For now, they are old
and in need all your care
Just like they are children
they want you most there

You look at your elder
I know you all do
And sometimes
you say yourself

What has happened to you?

Where is the person
who loved me so dear?
You once stood beside me

But that persons not here

The one standing before you
is now feeble and gray
And may not remember
the person you are
for a day

Though anger and sadness
may find its way in
You gaze into their eyes
And your day
you begin

The love and the care
Unconditional shown
is yours now to Give

Claim it
as your own

As you start your day
And care as you can
Remember with gladness
As you make your stand

Fight for the person
who gave you this life
And remember their struggles
Remember their strife

Even though they are failing
and it breaks your heart so

Remember they taught you
The way you should go

So, I say this to you
as it's often said to me

Don't wish them away

Forever is an Eternity

See

Waiting

So many things in our lives
we are waiting for

As children it's the holidays or our birthdays

Perhaps the birth of a sibling
To be that all important big brother or big sister

Then as we age

it's our first going to school

Then graduating for middle school to high school

Then from high school to college

For all of these transitions we learn to be patient and to
wait

Enduring all that comes with an air of grace that molds
us

As we grow
we too learn to wait for love

At first the wait is short
as our parents bestow upon us their undying love and
affection

As young people we wait to be loved by those around us
Letting us set out to choose or be chosen by one who
will carry our hearts and minds with them

But it's as we age that the waiting is more profound

We strive for employment to better our selves
Homes to shelter us
Partners to begin our lives anew

Then there is the waiting that is
Endless
That which comes for those who are past their prime
and now endure illness and longing

Their partners gone
They in the care of loved ones
Who with all good intentions
Bare their burdens tirelessly and without complaint
But see their struggles day to day

The waiting and want in an old one's eyes can at time
leave you breathless

You find yourself waiting for closure for them to see
their God and have the peace that they so rightly
deserve
No matter how right or wrong that may be

Then there is that lonely hour
That the waiting is finally coming to an end

Heartbroken and confused
Knowing that the world is going to change forever with
the closing of one's eyes

We are all waiting

For one thing or another

We are

Waiting

There are things that I've seen

There are things that I've seen
in this life of mine
That fill up my heart
and make my eyes shine

There are places and faces
And wonders
I've seen

And experiences aplenty
Of most I am keen

But the ones that have
caused me
to change most of all
are the ones that
cause sadness
and dark shadows to fall

Try as I may
to be light of heart
and be gay
Sometimes it is hard
to see life just this way

I've seen my dear family
in good times and bad
From joys of the birth of their children

to illnesses they've had
A range of emotions
I've shared too this day
But I stood there beside them
That is just my way

I've sailed on the oceans
A few chosen times
Seen islands of wonder
and heard music so fine

I've traveled the highways
Around this great land
I've seen soaring eagles
and have stood in the sand

From Jersey to Oahu
And Megan's Bay Too
Those are my treasures
I say this to you

I've watched in wide wonder
As death came to call
from family to friends
He visits us all

I've stood side by side
With grief in my heart
And a sense of such loss
it could tear you apart

But the one thing I know
I don't have here today

Is a sense of regret
In anytime or away

I have seen it in others
I say this is true
That lost inner look
Like there's nothing to do

That wish that you wish
if you did have a little more time
To just say those words
You could make it be fine

Like:

I'm sorry
I'm here
I'm lost and afraid
I try as I might and I need you to stay
Just a little more time
If there's only a way

So, with the things I have seen
Set deep in my heart
And the care and the love
You can't pull apart

I say to the ones
who may read this dear tale

If there is regret
Do this without fail

Tell the ones that you love
that love them each day

And when you don't see them
I miss you
you say

Hold close inside you
the ways that they are

For when they do leave

You

Forever's too far

From the first drop

From the first drop

to the last
This very life
goes by so fast

But it is our life

As we go on
our merry way
And live our lives
from day to day

The dance we do
from dawn to dusk
One hundred years
may seem enough

To live a life
a one so true

A masterpiece
just made for you

From infancy
To childhood fair
With love and trust
we learn to share

As young adults
we're taught
to sow
the seeds of work
so off we go

To labor as our elders have
To forge a way
That's not half bad

Soon families of
our own we share
We beam with pride
With our elders there

But time it's changing
As we know
Our young grow up
and off they go

Our elders too
begin to fade
As time and tide
take them away

And if it is so
I say to you
that
Fortune she does truly
smile on you

Live on well
from day to day
May cares be few
along the way
And joys like raindrops
grace your days

From first to last
may blessings be
Along with you
and family

So, it's true my tale I say
from
First drop till last
that is the way

Conversation

I hear you
I think to myself
Every word you say

I listen with great interest
to every word you say
But
It's that things that are never said
That make me sad of late

I wish that you could see me
As I come to call on you
And we used to carry on
Like the way some children do

But we have now our own lives
We gone our separate ways
But I still do long for those talks
in the good old days

Oh, there are still the messages
You send to me each day
Of the things that you are doing
And your travels bright and gay

But it's not that there is envy
Though sometimes those feeling's ring true
But it's for just your company

I long to be with you

So, as we
Us, siblings
get older
And I
your elder be
I wish that you be nearer

And come and chat with me

For of time
there is aplenty
And as we go on
you'll see

There are tales
and conversations

That I wish
you'd share with me

Too Angry to Pray

You said you'd always love me
You are proud of me you say

And now
when I gaze upon you
I'm even more lost than yesterday

You spoke to me of the seven things
that one day will be true
I now can see all of them
they're closing in
and
Getting far too close to you

First there is the anger that stands there in your way

Next there is the anguish that eats your heart away

Then there is denial

Oh no this can't be true

Then there is the loneliness that comes and tears at you

And then you claim you can rebuild
The world you used to know

And at last you believe acceptance is the way to go

You have also taught me to believe in:
"The One True God Above"
but tonight, I'm having a difficult time
My faith may need a shove

Oh no I cannot lose you
to the memory thief
or lose you in any other way

Our time it seems so brief

You have always been my playmate
My truest confidant
The keeper of my secrets
And the shield of all my wants

But now I am your champion
I will fight on in your stead
Lessons learned I shall carry
And with all the love that you have said

But tonight
It's true
I'm angry
Far too angry now to pray
For the things I know won't be mended
No matter what I say
Or
Whom I ask to make it so

So, I will lay here in the darkness
Teardrops coursing down my cheeks
No prayers tonight

But curses

You be damned
You awful memory thief